This book belongs to:

Astronaut _____

For Dad—you're always there for me, even when I can't see you —S. M.

For Baptiste, Floriane, and their little moons, Charlie & Willow —S. L.

For Deimos and Phobos, my distant cousins orbiting Mars —M.

Henry Holt and Company, *Publishers since 1866*
Henry Holt® is a registered trademark of Macmillan Publishing Group, LLC
175 Fifth Avenue, New York, NY 10010 • mackids.com

Library of Congress Cataloging-in-Publication Data
Names: McAnulty, Stacy, author. | Lewis, Stevie, illustrator.
Title: Moon! : Earth's best friend / Stacy McAnulty ; illustrated by Stevie Lewis.
Description: New York : Henry Holt and Company, [2019] | Series: Our universe
| Audience: Age 4–8. | Includes bibliographical references.
Identifiers: LCCN 2018054823 | ISBN 9781250199348 (hardcover)
Subjects: LCSH: Moon—Juvenile literature. | Solar system—Juvenile literature.
Classification: LCC QB582 .M3945 2019 | DDC 523.3—dc23
LC record available at https://lccn.loc.gov/2018054823

ISBN 978-1-250-23983-9 (special edition)

Our books may be purchased in bulk for promotional, educational, or business use. Please contact your local bookseller
or the Macmillan Corporate and Premium Sales Department at (800) 221-7945 ext. 5442 or by email at MacmillanSpecialMarkets@macmillan.com.

First edition, 2019 / Designed by Sophie Erb
The artist used colored pencils and digital tools to create the illustrations in this book.
Printed in China by RR Donnelley Asia Printing Solutions Ltd., Dongguan City, Guangdong Province
1 3 5 7 9 10 8 6 4 2

OUR UNIVERSE
MOON!
EARTH'S BEST FRIEND

BY Moon (**WITH STACY MCANULTY**)

ILLUSTRATED BY Moon (**AND STEVIE LEWIS**)

Henry Holt and Company ✳ New York

Look up. Look up! LOOK UP!
It's me. Moon!
I'm Earth's best friend.

Where Earth goes, I go.

We have been together since the beginning.
Almost. Let me tell you *our* story.
Once upon a time . . .

. . . about 4.5 billion years ago, a space rock
the size of Mars crashed into baby Earth. Big ole mess!

Pieces of rock, chunks of Earth, and even lava were blasted
into space. This crash trash came together to make ME!

A satellite!

Actually, I'm Earth's *only* natural satellite.

Natural: *not* created by Earthlings.

Satellite: I circle Earth.

She has thousands of
human-made satellites, too.
They're mostly metal and plastic.
Not exactly best-friend material.

Guess that makes me Earth's #1 *real* sidekick.

It takes me 27.3 days
to go around Earth once.

It also takes me 27.3 days
to spin once.

Coincidence?
I think not.

Means I'm dependable!

My face always smiles at Earth.
(You NEVER see my backside.)

But you probably noticed I look different every night.
Fun, right?

Check out
my PHASES!

waning
crescent

new
moon

waxing
crescent

last
quarter

waning
gibbous

full
moon

(Doesn't make
wolves howl.)

waxing
gibbous

first
quarter

Some other planets have best friends, too. I am MOON, but I'm not the only moon in the solar system.

NEPTUNE and moons

SATURN and moons

JUPITER and moons

MARS and moons

URANUS and moons

IO

CALLISTO

TITAN

GANYMEDE

Of all the moons,
I'm fifth biggest!

I'll always be Earth's pal, but that doesn't mean we're twinsies.

She's bigger.
Four times bigger!

6,784 miles around

24,874 miles around

And her gravity is six times stronger.

Gravity: the invisible force that makes an apple fall to the ground instead of flying up to the sky.

600

100

A cow that weighs 600 pounds on Earth would weigh only 100 pounds on me.

Speaking of cows . . .

Earth has cows.
And nursery rhymes.
And nursery rhymes starring cows.

But a cow has never jumped over me. I'm too far away for even a kangaroo to make that leap.

Average distance between Earth and me: 238,855 miles.

You could fit 30 Earths in that distance.
And probably a gazillion cows.

BFFs help each other out.

I keep Earth from being too wobbly.
This might be the most important thing I do,
and you probably didn't even know about it!

With me: gentle spinning.

My gravity at work!

Without me: topsy turvy.
Don't worry, Moon Gazers.
You're never without me.

I don't disappear during the day.
I'm always here for Earth.

You just can't see me
when it's super bright out,
or when it's cloudy, or when I'm
on the other side of Earth.

I can prove I'm always here.
Check out the oceans' tides.

High tide. Happens twice a day.

Low tide. Happens twice a day.

That's gravity again—my gravity—pulling on Earth's oceans.

I have the best views of Earth.
And Earth has the best views of me.

But some Earthlings
wanted to see me
up close.

I'm the only other place *in the universe*
where man has set foot. And I do mean MAN.
I'm still waiting for my first female astronaut.

I've had twelve moonwalkers,
and a few left footprints.

And some of those
footprints are still here!

No wind or rain or snow to mess them up.

Other things you won't find on me:

oxygen

mosquitoes (Which is a good thing, I think.)

liquid water

plants

animals

(including cows)

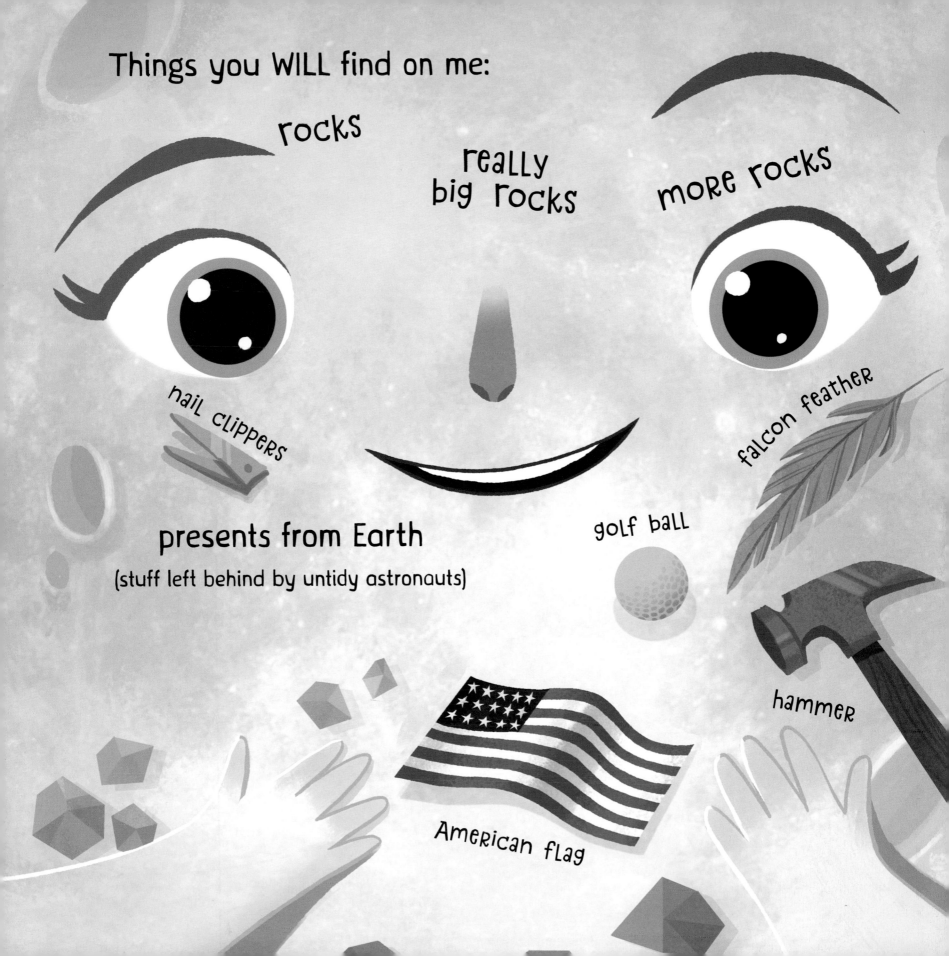

Earth and I have so much fun together!
Like when we play eclipse.

SOLAR ECLIPSE! I hide Sun for a few minutes.
We play this during the day.

LUNAR ECLIPSE! Earth's shadow passes over me.

We play this at night.

I'm always here for Earth.
I'm always here for you.
Where Earth goes, I go.

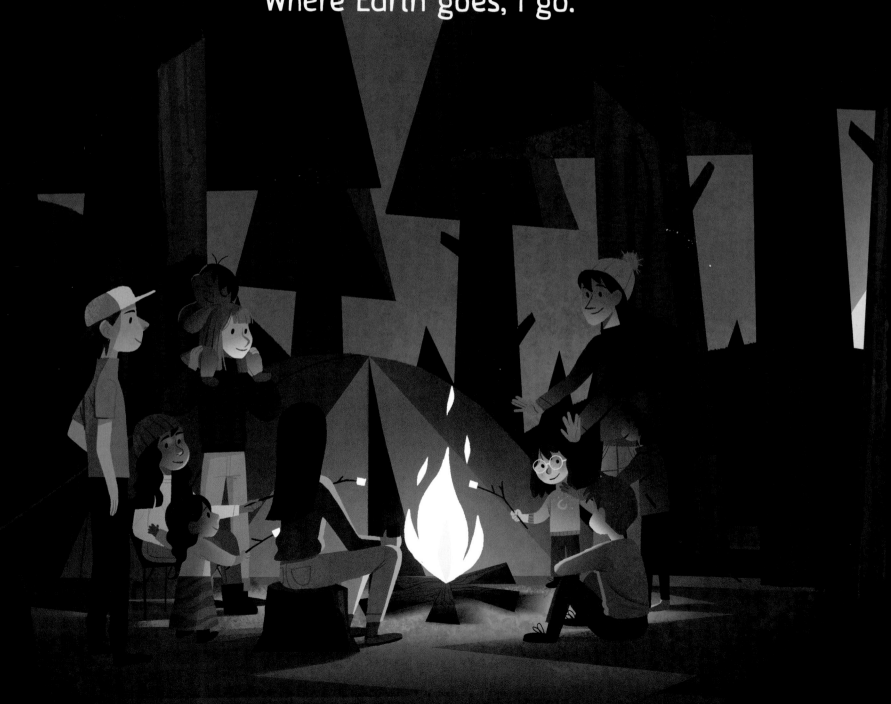

And where Earth goes, you go!
Guess that makes us
best friends, too.

Dear Fellow Moon Gazers,

It's easy to see why Moon is Earth's best friend. Moon is loyal. We know exactly where and when we'll see her. Moon is helpful. She keeps our planet from being too wobbly and creates the tides. She's fun. You can't have an eclipse without her. In addition, Earth and Moon have history. They go back about 4.5 billion years. So next time you see your BFF, say, "You're as marvelous as the Moon!" And that's quite the compliment.

Sincerely,

Stacy McAnulty

Author and fan of natural satellites

P.S. Every day, scientists are learning more and more about our solar system. (Yay, science!) So some details may change as our knowledge expands. But hey, that's to be expected. Right?

Two Truths and a Myth with Moon

Can you guess which two statements about me are true and which one is not?

Round 1

A. Wolves and dogs howl at me.
B. I'm moving farther away from Earth.
C. I have an iron-rich core at my center.

Answer:

B and C are true. On average, I'm approximately 238,855 miles from Earth. Every year, I move about an inch farther away. And like Earth, I have layers—crust, mantle, and core.

That means A is the myth. Even when I'm full, animals do not howl at me. But because I reflect so much more light when I'm full, animals can be more active at night.

Round 2

A. Twelve men have stepped on my surface.
B. I'm made of cheese.
C. I affect the oceans' tides.

Answer:

Of course B is a myth. About 500 years ago, playwright John Heywood joked, "The moone is made of a greene cheese." And it seems the rumor has been alive and well ever since. My Swiss cheese–look comes from craters made by space rocks (asteroids and meteors) crashing into me.

A and C are true. NASA has sent twelve astronauts for brief moonwalks. All were American men. And my gravity does pull on Earth's oceans, which creates the tides.

Round 3

A. Earthlings always see the same side of me.
B. I belong to no Earthling.
C. I make Earthlings crazy.

Answer:

Both A and B are facts. Because I rotate and revolve at the same speed, you're always gazing at the same hemisphere. However, I don't have a "dark side." Sun's light does shine on all parts of me, just at different times. Half of Earth is always lit by Sun; half of me is always lit, too. And I don't belong to anyone. A 1967 international treaty prohibits any nation or person or business from owning any natural objects in space.

The myth about me making people crazy is just . . . well, crazy. I also cannot help you fall in love or turn your friend into a werewolf. My influence is limited.

MOON by the Numbers

29.5 — We have a full moon every 29.5 Earth days. (The sidereal period is 27.3 days and the synodic period is 29.5 days.)

238,855 — The average distance between Earth and Moon is 238,855 miles.

260 — The temperature on the Moon can get up to 260°F.

-280 — And the temp can fall to -280°F.

2,160 — The diameter across Moon's equator is 2,160 miles.

2,157 — The diameter across Moon's poles is 2,157 miles. (She's not a perfect sphere.)

27.3 — One "year" on Moon would take 27.3 Earth days, if you consider a year to be how long it takes Moon to orbit Earth.

27.3 — One "day" on Moon would take 27.3 Earth days, if you consider a day to be how long it takes Moon to spin around once.

ALL in a Name

Blood Moon: This happens during a lunar eclipse as Moon passes through Earth's shadow and Moon appears red.

Blue Moon: The second full moon in one calendar month.

Micromoon: Since Moon does not orbit Earth in a perfect circle, sometimes she is a bit farther away and appears smaller. A micromoon happens when Moon is at her farthest from Earth.

Supermoon: The opposite of a micromoon. When Moon is full and at her closest to Earth, she will appear larger (by about 14 percent) and brighter (by about 30 percent).

Native cultures have also given names to Moon depending on the time of year. For example, the first full moon of the year has been called Wolf Moon, Old Moon, or Ice Moon. These names have more to do with life on Earth than the activities of Moon. Other cool names include Snow Moon, Harvest Moon, Strawberry Moon, Beaver Moon, and Thunder Moon.

Sources

Goldsmith, Mike, Margaret Hynes, and Barbara Taylor. *Earth and Space: A Thrilling Adventure from Planet Earth into the Universe*. New York: Kingfisher, 2016.

Kerrod, Robin. *Universe*. Eyewitness Books. New York: DK Publishing, 2015.

Mancini, Mark. "Why Do People Say the Moon Is Made of Cheese?" Mental Floss, Oct. 16, 2018. mentalfloss.com/article/53107/why-do-people-say-moon-made-cheese.

NASA. "A Compilation of Human Artifacts on the Moon." Maps and catalog, July 5, 2012. history.nasa.gov/humanartifacts.html.

NASA Science. "Earth's Moon: Our Natural Satellite." Updated Oct. 5, 2018. solarsystem.nasa.gov/moons/earths-moon/overview/.

National Geographic. "Full Moon Names, Explained." Updated Oct. 24, 2018. nationalgeographic.com/science/space/solar-system/full-moon/.

Trefil, James. *Space Atlas: Mapping the Universe and Beyond*. Washington, DC: National Geographic, 2012.